# Victorious Living Prayer Guide

Dr. Genet Azang-Njaah

ISBN: 978-1-947662-94-0

Library of congress number: 2020907258

# Table of Contents

# DEDICATION

This book is dedicated to my beloved husband, Lucas Azang-Njaah- You have taught me how to stand firm. Thank you for loving the real me and our children.

To my beloved children, Mbong and her husband, Mark, Ndang, and Sanglui, and to my grandchildren, Isabelle and Oliver Henry, I love you with all my heart! Thank you for giving me an opportunity to grow in my walk with God. You made me discover the hidden riches of God in earthen vessels as I labored for you day and night in prayer.

# Acknowledgments

To my Siblings in Cameroon, your love will never depart from me. Let this book inspire your life.

To SisterPal women- You have inspired me to write this book, thank you, our hearts remain knitted together in God's love. Continue with what you have learned from our Lord and pass them on.

To my beloved mother, Monica Ngong, I will never forget you lifting up your voice to God in prayer. Thank you for dedicating your entire life to your husband and children.

To my beloved father, Prince Alexander Ndi Ngong, who is now with the Lord, I am so thankful for having you as my dad. Your love for me empowered me to be who I am today. You introduced me to Missions and it has transformed my life. You are my hero!

To my beloved Pastor, Steven Badorf, and his family: We are forever grateful for having you in our lives. Thank you for passing on this knowledge of our Lord and Savior to the world.

To my Church family, Kirkridge Presbyterian, thank you for loving us. We truly appreciate your support. Special thanks to Retired Reverend Biddle Foster and his wife Vivian Foster, who played the role of grandparents when our children were young.

To CBC Women's Union- USA, thank you for allowing me to grow in my walk with the Lord, during the time I serve as a guest speaker for retreats, conferences and also as one of your community leaders.

To my friend and beloved sister, Patience Ngalla, thank you for your sacrificial love for Jesus and for joining me in praying for our families, women, churches and nations. God has answered our prayers with the 2020 Vision.

To Reverend Thomas Hyndman, who served as a Spiritual Leader, during our first mission project to International students in the Washington Metropolitan Area in 1991. Thank you for all your incredible work with internationals. Thank you for providing a venue for our meetings!

To IEM PRESS and editors, thank you for your love for Jesus!

And to Dr. Eric Tangumonkem, thank you immensely for the countless hours you put into this book. Thank you for encouraging me to write!

To all: Let God meet you in such a time like this when the world is in chaos. He is a God of peace and comfort. He is a perfect Healer and the Restorer of all nations. Cry to Him, run to Him with your problems, speak with him daily, read his word. Listen to him and obey His voice, and He will raise up an army to fight your battles. He will provide a provider to meet all your needs. He will bring justice to your case. Trust and see what He can and will do for you.

This book is about you and your relationship with God. He knows your name and the number of hairs on your head! He created you in His image and for his glory! He has won your battle, so stand firm and move on with what He tells you to do.

# Foreword

"And what you have heard from me in the
presence of many witnesses entrust to faithful
men (and women), who will be able to teach
others also."—2 Timothy 2:2 (ESV)

From the time God warms our hearts and saves us
giving us faith in Christ Jesus till the day we meet
our Savior face-to-face, Christians are encour-
aged to grow. One of the most important means
of growth that God has given us is prayer. God
intentionally made us in his image and created us
for relationship with Himself. As human beings,
we communicate all the time, but do we communicate with God? It's through prayer that we
can establish and grow in our relationship with
God and the Lord Jesus as we take our needs
and the pains of this world to the only person
who can help and do anything about them. Yet
many Christians claim that they don't know how
to pray. How should they begin their prayers?
What should the content of their prayers be?
And how should they end their prayers? Should
their prayers be short? Or should their prayers
be long? These are all legitimate concerns and
valid questions. Even the twelve disciples, who
spent three years with Jesus himself, begged Jesus
to teach them to pray.

After learning how to pray and then spending many years actively praying, Dr. Genet Azang-Njaah imparts her understanding in this book so that you can gain from what she has learned and grow in your own personal relationship with God too. Take this book and read it, but even more importantly, take this book and pray. Apply these Scriptures and these principles. Put them into practice and grow in your own relationship with the Lord Jesus Christ. Then pass them on to someone else. Teach them to pray too that we might all grow up in the grace and knowledge of the Lord Jesus Christ.

Under the Mercy,
Steven Badorf
Pastor,
Kirkridge Presbyterian Church, ARP

# Statement from My Husband

To my Beloved wife and best friend,

Thank you for obeying God's call to assist Christians of all levels with a Victorious Living Prayer Guide. This book will facilitate their communication with God Almighty, the Great Communicator. Christ advised his disciples to pray succinctly with purposeful driven prayers. This book is filled with selected Bible verses and sample prayers to enable each reader pray more effectively in any given situation. It can be used as a devotional or a guide for a group bible study.

Lucas Azang-Njaah, Elder: Associate Reformed Presbyterian Church, Manchester, MD. USA

# Introduction

**Pray in the Spirit at all times and
on every occasion. Stay alert and
be persistent in your prayers for all
believers everywhere. —*Ephesians 6:18***

As a Christian you need to learn and know how to pray effectively. There are all kinds of prayers in the Bible, and we have provided you with some verses to enable you to pray more effectively. The entire book is full of scriptures to apply to your situation as you pray daily; when you pray, use the name of Jesus, because he has given his followers all power and authority to bind and loose things on earth. *Matthew 16:19.* Jesus said, "For where two or three are gathered in His name, He is present with them. *Matthew 18:20.* You have made the most important decision of your life to schedule time to pray. Our Lord Jesus Christ gave a mandate to pray and to share Him with others. Jesus admonished us to watch and pray so that we won't fall into temptation. *Matthew 26:41.*

The privilege of every child of God is to "come boldly to His throne to obtain mercy and grace in time of need." *Hebrews 4: 14-16*. The effectual fervent prayer of a righteous man availeth much. *James 5:16*. Come to him and let him know how you feel. He is waiting for your sweet voice and your thoughts about Him, his world and any problem you have.

# Chapter One
# How Jesus Prayed

*"To every soul that knows how to pray, to every soul that by faith comes to Jesus, the true mercy seat, divine sovereignty wears no dark and terrible aspect but is full of love."* —**Charles Spurgeon**

You can follow His examples to learn how to pray: When we speak, laugh, cry, yell, ask, shout, sing and even when we are silent, we are communicating. Let us observe how Christ communicated with His father:

- Jesus prayed in secluded places, and sometimes He got up early in the morning to pray. *Mark 1:35, Matthew 14:23*
- He prayed during His baptism. *Luke 3:21-22*
- He prayed in the wilderness. *Luke 5:16*
- He went off on the mountains to pray, praying all night. *Luke 6:12*
- He prayed for His disciples. *John 17:1-25*
- He praised His Father. *Luke 10:21*
- He thanked His Father. *Mark 14:22*
- He thanked His Father before raising Lazarus from the dead. *John 11:41-42*

- He obeyed His Father and was submissive to the Cross. *Matthew 26:39*
- He prayed before his arrest. *Luke 22:39-46*
- He cried out to His father. *Matthew 27:46*
- He taught His followers how to pray. *Luke 11:1, Matthew 6: 5-15*
- He blessed children. *Matthew 19:13*
- He prayed for food before feeding the five-thousand. *Matthew 14:19*
- He taught his disciples to pray using His name. *John 16:26*
- He was led by the Holy Spirit to fast, so He fasted for forty days and forty nights. *Matthew 4:1-11*
- Christ prayed in the garden of Gethsemane for God's will to be done in His life. *Matthew 26:42, Mark 14:32-39*
- He asked his father to *forgive* those who were cursing and killing him. *Luke 23: 34*
- He spoke a word on the cross to a thief, *"today you will be with me in paradise"*. *Luke 23:43*

What a privilege to come before God through Jesus, taking our problems to Him, *just as we are.*

**Personal Reflection:**

1.  **During your study time how many things did you learn from how Jesus prayed?**

2.  **During what events did Jesus pray?**

3.  **Why did Jesus pray during each event?**

# Chapter Two

# Prayers during Spiritual Warfare

*"You have to expect spiritual warfare whenever you stand up for righteousness or call attention to basic values. It's just a matter of light battling the darkness. But the light wins every time. You can't throw enough darkness on light to put it out."* —**Thomas Kinkade**

The Bible commands Christians to pray without ceasing. 1 Thessalonians *5:16*. Spiritual warfare is real, as Paul tells us, "For we wrestle not against flesh and blood, but against principalities, against powers, against the rulers of the darkness of this world, against spiritual wickedness in high places." *Ephesians 6:11-17*. The Armor of God is a Believer's (PPE) Personal protective equipment during warfare. Paul vividly describes the purpose of each part in Ephesians chapter 6. This warfare involves principalities, powers, spiritual wickedness and systems - these are the things placed on our nations, homes, families, children, and places of work to combat our walk with the Lord. As children of God, we have the power to go to God with any problem we have! He is *I AM*, *Almighty* and *Omnipotent*, and He will fight the battle for us. *Exodus 3:14, Revelations 19:6, Exodus 14:14, Psalms 91:15.*

Christ said that when we pray, we should go to our room, close the door, and pray to Him in private; His Father who sees in private will reward us in public. *Matthew 6:6.* Most individuals are going through stormy lives and relationships. The enemy may distract you with warfare in such a manner that you cannot focus or maximize your God-given potential. Jesus said, "Come unto me and you will find rest for your soul." *Matthew 11:28.* Let us go to Christ together and we will find rest for our souls. We need rest because our world is full of unrest. Christ is the answer. He is patiently waiting for us. His peace is divine and cannot be bought in any Super- Market or Wall Street! He is your Peace and Rest!

Being victorious in your prayer life leads to a victorious life in all other aspects. Jesus wants us to understand that He has overcome the world. *John. 16:16-33*. He came that we may have life and have it abundantly, but the thief comes to kill, steal, and destroy. *John 10:10*.

The weapons of our warfare are not carnal but *mighty through God* to the pulling down of strongholds. *2 Corinthians 10:3-5*. We can't fight spiritual battles with fleshly weapons, and our prayer life will reveal the type of weapons we need for spiritual combat. In *Isaiah 54:17*, God told His children that no weapon formed against them would prosper, and when Daniel prayed, the Prince of Persia resisted him for 21 days. *Daniel 10:13*. Persistent prayers will open doors to *answered prayers*. Some examples of spiritual warfare are- Problems with anger and rage, hatred, problems with marriages , unforgiveness, financial issues, broken homes, obstacles in education, problems with relationships, hidden obstacles in the society to hinder your progress, not knowing your identity, not knowing your history, believing a lie, spiritual and financial oppression. These are some examples of strongholds used by the enemy. We must learn how to pray using scriptures to demolish strongholds. *Then, whatever we bind on earth will be bound in heaven, and whatever we loose on earth will be loosed in heaven.*

*Matthew 18:18. When we* resist the devil, he will flee from us. *James 4:7.*

*Our enemy, the devil, prowls around like a roaring lion looking for someone to devour. Resist him, standing firm in the faith. 1 Peter 5:8-9.*

*Be constant in prayers like Anna, the prophetess, who spent her days on earth praying in the temple. Luke 2:36-38.*

- Pray prayers that will move mountains. *Mark 11:23.*
- Pray prayers that move the heart of God: *Isaiah 1:18, Luke 1:8-16, Luke 1:59-66*
- When you pray speak with God as Abraham did. *Genesis 18:25-26.*
- Trust the Lord as Mary did. *Luke 1:38.*
- Cry to Christ and you will be healed like the woman with the issue of blood. *Luke 8:43-47.*
- Ask God to heal you using medications and medicinal plants. *Genesis 1:29, Ezekiel 47:12, John 9:5-7.*
- Ask God to use you in ending the sin of racism in our nation. Racism is an attack on God's character. God doesn't show partiality. *Romans 2:11*

*Prayer will reveal the sinfulness of our hearts and enable us to tear down pillars of racism.*

**Gather three to five individuals in your church or community; choose a category for which to pray weekly.**

# Chapter Three
# Prayers for Women

*"Do you often feel like parched ground, unable to produce anything worthwhile? I do. When I am in need of refreshment, it isn't easy to think of the needs of others. But I have found that if, instead of praying for my own comfort and satisfaction, I ask the Lord to enable me to give to others, an amazing thing often happens - I find my own needs wonderfully met. Refreshment comes in ways I would never have thought of, both for others, and then, incidentally, for myself."* —**Elisabeth Elliot**

Woman, you are the most influential person in your home. Genesis 2:22, God brought you to your husband. You set the emotional thermostat in your home!

When praying for women, we should ask the Lord for the following:

- Women will learn to pray for their children and husbands.
- She will collaborate with God to be a suitable helpmate.
- She will become the intercessor for the home God created for man, and woman for His glory.

- The woman was created for the glory of God- you are the backbone of society.
- Women will discover their calling and obey God's voice.
- She will make Jesus the Lord of her life.
- Women should have opportunities to be financially viable, caring for themselves and their children.

- Women should learn how to manage their families and homes.
- Pregnant women will protect their babies in the womb from drugs, alcohol, and cigarettes.
- Women will understand the power of motherhood.
- Women will make time to teach their children.

- The woman should understand the effect of the power of her tongue on her children.
- The woman's body is the temple of the Most High.
-  Her tongue and her womb are sacred organs before God.
- Women produce kings, queens, presidents and all leaders.
- Women should understand the power to call on God.
- Women should understand that their purpose on earth is to influence the next generation.

*Woman, know that you can change the entire universe with your words, action and love. The bond between you and your child sets the atmosphere for the next generation. Curses or blessings will follow your children based on the words you used on them.*

*What seeds are you planting in your home? As you pray, let God reveal them to you.*

*Read (Proverbs 31)*

**Gather three to five individuals in your church or community; choose a category for which to pray weekly.**

# Chapter Four
# Prayers for Men

*"We should not pray for God to be on our side, but pray that we may be on God's side."* —**Billy Graham**

***Jeremiah 1:5 ~ James 4:10, Genesis 2:7~Genesis 1:26***

- Do you know your identity? You are God's masterpiece. *Ephesians 2:10.*
- Created by God's own hands. He molded and formed you in His image.
- You determine the vision for your family; A family without a vision will not succeed in life. *Proverbs 29:18.* So, the man should teach his wife and children what God has revealed to him about family life. "The

Lord said, write it down, make it clear so that everyone can read it quickly." *Habakkuk 2:2*. When praying for men we should consider the following;

- Pray that men should understand their responsibilities as husbands and fathers.
- Men should obey God's word for their calling.
- Men are to protect their families. *Colossians 3:19*. Love must protect the individual.
- Men are to love their wives as their own bodies. *Ephesians 5:28*
- A man must provide for his family. *1 Timothy 5:8*
- A man must have the knowledge of God's purpose for him regarding his marriage.
- Men should pray for protection for marriages - and the role of in-laws.

Pray that men will understand the concept of oneness in marriage. *Mark 10:8*. The man will understand when Goliath is living in his home. Men will be spiritual leaders of their families.

*1 Timothy 3:2, Titus 1:7-14*. Men should avoid adulteress women. *Proverbs 7*.

Pray for the man to identify unsaved family members and their effect upon marriage.

**Key points for men to identify:** Inappropriate alerts from devices can be poisonous arrows, used by the enemy to dissolve marriages, dissolve the power of obedience and destroy our children. As leaders, men should be able to identify anyone whose character is like, Judas Iscariot and let God reveal the enemy's strategies to make men captives.

## Men's Prayers for the Parent-Child Relationship

The glory of children is their father. *Proverbs 17:6.* Fathers, your relationship with your children determine their success in life. Pray that parents will understand the power of the tongue on a child. Do you curse or bless your children? Children are gifts from the Lord. *Psalms 127:3*

The LORD your God, am a jealous God, punishing the children for the sin of the fathers to the third and fourth generation of those who hate me, but showing love to a thousand generations of those who love me and keep my commandments. *Exodus 20:5-6*

*Deuteronomy 24:16* - Fathers shall not be put to death for their children, nor children put to death for their fathers; each is to die for his own sin. --pray for deliverance from the sin of alcoholism, pornography and substance abuse.

*Proverbs 22:6* - Train up a child in the way he should go, and when he is old, he will not depart from it.

*Ephesians 6:4* - And you, *fathers,* do not provoke your children to wrath, but bring them up in the training and admonition of the Lord.

- Men should pray for their children's salvation, vocations, spouses, and calling in life. *Psalms 1, Proverbs 7, Proverbs 5:7*
- Men should pray for their own salvation, for them to stay away from evil friends - the path that leads to destruction. *Psalms 1*
- Men should pray for protection, and guidance to pursue their God-given purpose in life. *Genesis 1:27-28, Isaiah 44:2*

- Men should intercede daily for their children and wives. *1 Corinthians 15:33*
- Men should intervene for their children to be drug-free. *1 Corinthians 15:33*

## Reflection for men:

Who was your role model?

Who impacted your life?

Every man is a leader. A leader is one who moves people forward.

Who do you lead?

What is your legacy to the next generation? You have been empowered by God to lead the world. So, do what is right before God by standing up for your family.

# Chapter Five

# Prayers for Pastors and Church Leaders

*"Prayer makes a godly man, and puts within him the mind of Christ, the mind of humility, of self-surrender, of service, of pity, and of prayer. If we really pray, we will become more like God, or else we will quit praying."*
**—E.M. Bounds**

*Psalms 28:7 ~ Psalms 118:7-14 ~ Psalms 144:1-2 ~ 1 Timothy 2:1-3 ~ James 1:5-6 ~ Numbers 6:24-26 ~ Psalms 5:11-12 ~Matthew 21:13*

Pray for your pastor, his wife, and his children; they are the first line of attack from the enemy. Pray for their protection and safety, pray that God will be your pastor's rock, his shield, his deliverer, and his refuge. Pastors are called to preach the good news and not false messages, so pray that God gives your pastor wisdom and a spirit of discernment in the church that he shepherds (he should be a true shepherd to his flock.) Pray that the church will repent of any sin against God's Word.

Pray for Elders, Deacons and those in authority in your church. The spiritual growth of the Elders will have an impact in the church of Christ. Pray for a training program for elders and leaders in your church. Pray for the effectiveness of the Gospel and for the church to be a true blessing to those who visit each Sunday. Pray for missionaries from local churches who are stationed around the world. "And Jesus declared to them, "It is written: "My house will be called the house of prayer." But you are making it to be a den of robbers". *Matthew 21:13.* God's house is for everyone- for all nations- you are welcome- He created every race, tribe, and tongue for His glory! If you believe in him, you will enjoy His blessings.

*Gather three to five individuals in your church or community; choose a category for which to pray weekly.*

# Chapter Six

# Prayers for Our Nations, Orphans, and Widows

*"The more praying there is in the world, the better the world will be; the mightier the forces against evil everywhere."* —**E.M. Bounds**

*2 Chronicles 7:14 ~ Proverbs 21:1 ~ Proverbs 11:14 ~ Psalms 74:17 ~ Psalms 24:1 ~ 1 Corinthians 10:26 ~ 1Timothy 2:1-2 ~ Romans 13:1 ~ Jeremiah 29:7 ~ Esther 4:3-17~ Nehemiah Chapter 1*

Moses interceded for the nation of Israel. *Exodus 32:7-14, Exodus 30-33.*

- Read Exodus 32:7-14 and observe how Moses prayed for his nation. He pleaded with God and asked him to turn from his anger and stop the destruction of his people, God listened to Moses and changed his mind. Follow Moses's example on how you can pray for your nation.

- Nehemiah interceded for his nation. Confessing the sins of his nation, himself and his family, he stated "we have acted very wickedly towards you (God.) We have not obeyed your commands, decrees and laws." (*Nehemiah 1:6-7*) Nehemiah didn't exempt himself from the sins of his nation and family. Nehemiah chapter 1 will enhance your spiritual growth.
- God says, if my people, who are called by my name, will humble themselves and pray and seek my face and turn from their wicked ways, then I will hear from heaven, and I will forgive their sin and will heal their land. *2 Chronicles 7:14*.
- You can stand in the gap for your nation against the sin of annihilation of citizens for such a time like this as Queen Esther.
- The king's heart is a stream of water in the hand of the Lord; he turns it wherever he will. *Proverbs 21:1*.
- For lack of guidance, a nation falls, but victory is won through many advisers. *Proverbs 11:14*.

- Show proper respect to everyone, love the family of believers, fear God, and honor the emperor. *1 Peter 2:17.*
- Let everyone be subject to the governing authorities, for there is no authority except that which God has established. *Romans 13:1. (The authorities that exist have been established by God.)*
- I urge you then, first, that petitions, prayers, intercession and thanksgiving be made for all people - for kings and all those in authority, that we may live peaceful and quiet lives in all godliness and holiness. *1 Timothy 2:1-2 (NIV)*

**What are the sins of your nation?**
- The nation of Israel was oppressed by the sin of slavery
- Oppression of God's people
- Financial oppression
- Attack on family life
- Annihilation of unborn children and citizens
- Spiritual wickedness in high places- *Tear down the pillars of rebellion against God in your homes, relationships and nation. Taking action now by teaching your children to fear God and do what is right, so God will not visit the sins of the parents on the children to the 3rd to 4th generations. Numbers 14:18.*

God is holy and He created this world for his glory. Man was given dominion to rule the world, however due to the presence of sin, man has misused his God-given power and become greedy.

- Pray against the sin of corruption.
- Pray against the sin of deceit- This is the 9th commandment.
- Pray against human and child sacrifices: -*Leviticus 18:21, Leviticus 20:3 and Deuteronomy 12:30-31, Psalms 106:3.*

Choose any nation - from A through Z - and pray for the leaders, beginning with the president, senator, congress, all branches of government - including the governors, mayors, council members, businesses in local communities, institutions, military, police officers, and homes. It is easy to break down prayers into communities such as homes, parents, educators, and lawmakers.

Pray for deliverance for those in captivity or oppression, opioid and pleasure epidemics, or slaves to instant gratification. *Ephesians 6.* Finally, pray for teachers, professionals, healthcare workers, and the sick.

**Students**: Pray for wisdom, focus and success.

Pray for **farmers**: for protection as they provide for their communities:

**Place of work**: Pray for peace, patience and respect for all at work. Pray for those in authority-managers and supervisors! Man was created to work. Whatsoever ye do, do it with all your heart, as to the Lord and not unto men. *Colossians 3:23-24. God will bless you as you bless others at work.*

### Prayers for Widows and Orphans
### *James 1:27 ~ Deuteronomy 14:28-29*
Pray for hope and comfort for all who are grieving.

- New homes for orphans and the homeless.
- Pray for the underprivileged all over the world for God to provide and fight for them.

**Deliverance from temptation:** *Matthew 4.* Read the chapter, observing how Jesus dealt with temptations from the enemy. This passage reveals the basic concept of all temptations. The devil uses the lust of the eyes, flesh and pride of life to attack believers. When Christ was faced with any temptation, he quoted scriptures to combat the enemy.

**Deliverance from captivity:** *Ephesians 6:11-17.* Take a look at a picture of a biblical Roman soldier with an armor – the helmet, the shield, the belt, the sword etc., use it as a tool to combat any captivity in your life. Tear down all thoughts and argument against God's word… *2Corinthians 10:5*

**Deliverance from debt:**
The love of money is the root of all evil. It is easier for a camel to go through the eye of a needle than for a rich man to enter the kingdom of God. *Matthew 19:24.*

- Owe no one anything except love. *Romans 13:8*
- The rich rule over the poor and the borrower is slave to the lender. *Proverbs 22:7, Psalms 37: 21, 1 Timothy 6:10.*

No one knows how to pray perfectly - *but every prayer counts before God*, and He listens to all His children. The Lord's Prayer is our model to learn how to pray. We are commanded by Paul to pray always with all prayer and supplication in the Spirit. *Ephesians 6:18*

*Gather three to five individuals in your church or community; choose a category for which to pray weekly.*

# Chapter Seven
# The Samaritan Woman

*"When you find your definitions in God, you find the very purpose for which you were created. Put your hand into God's hand, know His absolutes, demonstrate His love, present His truth, and the message of redemption and transformation will take hold".* —**Ravi Zacharias**

*Bible Reading: John 4:7-36 (ESV)*

[7] *A woman from Samaria came to draw water. Jesus said to her, "Give me a drink."* [8] *(For his disciples had gone away into the city to buy food.)* [9] *The Samaritan woman said to him, "How is it that you, a Jew, ask for a drink from me, a woman of Samaria?" (For Jews have no dealings with Samaritans.)* [10] *Jesus answered her, "If you knew the gift of God, and who it is that is saying to you, 'Give me a drink,' you would have asked him, and he would have given you living water."* [11] *The woman said to him, "Sir, you have nothing to draw water with, and the well is deep. Where do you get that living water?* [12] *Are you greater than our father Jacob? He gave us the well and drank from it himself, as did his sons and his livestock."* [13] *Jesus said to her, "Everyone who drinks of this water will be thirsty again,* [14] *but whoever drinks of the water that I will give him will never be thirsty again. The water that I will give him will become in him a spring of water welling up to*

eternal life." [15] The woman said to him, "Sir, give me this water, so that I will not be thirsty or have to come here to draw water."

[16] Jesus said to her, "Go, call your husband, and come here." [17] The woman answered him, "I have no husband." Jesus said to her, "You are right in saying, 'I have no husband'; [18] for you have had five husbands, and the one you now have is not your husband. What you have said is true." [19] The woman said to him, "Sir, I perceive that you are a prophet. [20] Our fathers worshiped on this mountain, but you say that in Jerusalem is the place where people ought to worship." [21] Jesus said to her, "Woman, believe me, the hour is coming when neither on this mountain nor in Jerusalem will you worship the Father. [22] You worship what you do not know; we worship what we know, for salvation is from the Jews. [23] But the hour is coming, and is now here, when the true worshipers will worship the Father in spirit and truth, for the Father is seeking such people to worship him. [24] God is spirit, and those who worship him must worship in spirit and truth." [25] The woman said to him, "I know that Messiah is coming (he who is called Christ). When he comes, he will tell us all things." [26] Jesus said to her, "I who speak to you am he."

[27] Just then his disciples came back. They marveled that he was talking with a woman, but no one said, "What do you seek?" or, "Why are you talking with her?" [28] So the

*woman left her water jar and went away into town and said to the people,* [29] *"Come, see a man who told me all that I ever did. Can this be the Christ?"* [30] *They went out of the town and were coming to him.*

[31] *Meanwhile the disciples were urging him, saying, "Rabbi, eat."* [32] *But he said to them, "I have food to eat that you do not know about."* [33] *So the disciples said to one another, "Has anyone brought him something to eat?"* [34] *Jesus said to them, "My food is to do the will of him who sent me and to accomplish his work.* [35] *Do you not say, 'There are yet four months, then comes the harvest'? Look, I tell you, lift up your eyes, and see that the fields are white for harvest.* [36] *Already the one who reaps is receiving wages and gathering fruit for eternal life, so that sower and reaper may rejoice together.*

### Let this story assist us as we interact with others in prayer.

**Discussion**: I love the story of the Samaritan woman because it encompasses many issues related to men and women today. During Jesus times, Samaritans were regarded as outcasts in their society. Samaritans and Jews were two different groups of people who hated each other. *(Verses 9-10)* Jews who had intermarried with Gentiles were considered "untouchables."

What can we learn from this story? The first lesson is that Christ had to deal with individuals who were biased against others.

The second lesson: Jesus intentionally went through Samaria because He wanted His word to be heard there. He addressed the problem in the city - and the woman's lifestyle - by introducing His identity. What are the problems in our cities and nations today? How should we pray for them? The third lesson: Lifestyle - how is our lifestyle? Where do we hang out? The Samaritan woman represents *everyone*. We are not given her name, but she is clearly associated with her nation and the main production in the city (prostitution.) As Jesus traveled through Samaria to get to Galilee, He initiated the conversation, and based on the woman's response, He taught her and revealed Himself to her.

Jesus knew this woman had misused her God-given gift. He saw greatness in her and understood that if women encountered God, they would take their nation back. He knew that it was the seed of the woman who will crush the head of the enemy. *Genesis 3:15.*

Jesus took time to teach her because He came to *restore women*, knowing that it was a woman who was misled in the Garden of Eden and she still suffers from the consequences of that decision. Jesus came to rescue everyone from that sin! He knew that He must set this woman free from her bondage of prostitution because she was fashioned and created by God's own hand - created to be a blessing - not a curse. *Genesis 22-23.*

Remember, God couldn't rest until woman was created; He provisioned her with gifts and knowledge to bless her home, community, and nation. She must first be delivered before comprehending her potential. In the past, this woman's peers had encountered God, blessing their homes, communities and nations.

For example:

- Rahab collaborated with God's people and hid the Hebrew spies in her attic. *Joshua, Chapter 2.*
- Jochebed gave up everything and trusted God for the safety of her son, Moses. *Exodus 2:1-10.*
- Hannah fasted and prayed for a son who become Israel's prophet. (Samuel.) *1 Samuel 1:9-28.*
- Esther was placed in the palace and she saved her nation. *Esther 4.*

## One woman can make a difference - One man can make a difference.

No one should live in shame as the Samaritan woman. Christ knew that if this woman encountered Him, her nation would change, her city would change, her lifestyle would change, and the entire village would be set free from captivity. He knew that demonic strongholds would be broken, shattered dreams would be restored, and peace would reign in her life; husbands would be committed to their wives again. This woman had five husbands and she was in another relationship with a man she wasn't married to! This shows that satisfaction is not found in the number of husbands or wives we have. Christ knew that He must give this woman eternal life, that the blessings of Abraham must be extended to not only her, but to all who crossed her path.

Jesus knew this woman was lonely, evidenced by the unusual time in which she visited the well. The first question He asked: Was there water for Him to drink? *Drink?* Christ is the living water (*John 4:14*) and He introduced this concept to the woman in a manner she understood. Her problem was spiritual, not physical.

- *Give me a drink.* Yes, He was a Jew and she was an outcast, so, why did He want

52

a relationship with this group of people – *outcasts?* Salvation is for everyone who believes in Christ, every group, every tribe, and every nation. The blessings of God are for everyone. Pursuing happiness is for everyone. God created His world for everyone. God initiated the concept of creation. *Genesis 1:1*. He owns the entire world. We own nothing. *We own nothing.* We were born naked. *Job 1:21*

- As shown in the first chapter of Genesis, this woman is part of the power and dominion to rule her territory, so Christ made time to bring her soul into His kingdom. The pain of her shame is enormous, and even the righteous cannot be seen with this prostitute. Her nation is doomed, her identity is doomed, her village is doomed. She is alone, under a curse because of her lifestyle. Christ had to break this taboo, setting her free, knowing that she would be the one to share the gospel with her people. Remember: Christ came to set the captives free and to deliver those who are in bondage. He was born for this mission so he will not miss any opportunity to fulfil it. *Luke 4:18*.

- This woman's problem was sex and relationships; she was looking for *true love*.

Christ's last request of this woman was that she go and call her *husband.*

What is your problem today? Is it related to what you do, drink, or eat? Is your pain from your nation? Your city or village? Race? Relationships? Profession? Money? Financial crisis? Depression? Whatever it is, wherever it originates, Christ asks us to give it to him in exchange for living waters. In the above story, He reveals himself to the Samaritan woman as the "Messiah." He calls Himself the gift of God. If you hear the voice of the Living Waters speaking to you, know that *He is that gift of God.* He demands your worship. **God is spirit, and those who worship him must worship in spirit and truth." *John 4:24.* He is Truth! *John 17:17.***

*Are we walking in his truth?*

**When we encounter God, he changes us to become a blessing in our villages, communities, and nations.**

Our nation needs revival today. Where are our children? They are depressed and confused with mixed messages from their peers and the media. Parents are overwhelmed with this culture's demand on them and are parading in debts. Parents cannot pursue their God-given assignment for their families. Christ initiated his love to this woman and her village, showing mercy and forgiving her sins. Let this story enable you to pray according to your need.

# Chapter Eight
# PRAYER CHARTS

*"We must not sit still and look for miracles; up and doing, and the Lord will be with thee. Prayer and pains, through faith in Christ Jesus, will do anything."* —**George Eliot**

| Is there a problem in your life with unforgiveness? Action Plan! | | |
| --- | --- | --- |
| **Prayer Guide** | **Key scripture: Matthew 5:24** | **Notes** |
| **Topic: Problem with Forgiveness** | Leave your gift before the altar. First go and be reconciled to your brother; then come and offer your gift | Matthew 5:24 |
| Define forgiveness and why should you forgive? | A disciple asked Christ how many times should he forgive his brother who sins against him? Up to seven times? | Matthew 18:21 |

| | | |
|---|---|---|
| How many times should I forgive? | Christ answered, "I say unto you, not seven times but seven-ty-seven times seven" | Matthew 18: 22 |
| Is there a need for forgiveness in your relation-ships? Family, church, community? | Make a list of everyone you need to forgive. | |
| What is your action plan? | Ask God to help you with the spirit of unforgiveness. | Matthew 18:23 |
| Morning: | Choose a quiet place to pray<br><br>Read the story of the King who settled accounts with his Servants. Matthew 18:23-35. Duration of your prayer depends on the severity of the Problem. | Matthew 18:23-35 Matthew 6:12 |

| | | |
|---|---|---|
| Evening: Action Plan → | Did God Speak to you?<br>Did you obey him?<br><br>Conclude your prayer session with the following action plan using the three aspects of God's character; love, mercy and His grace. (Forgiveness by Douglas Connelly. Page,14.)<br><br>After concluding, call the person you have forgiven and bless them with a word from the Bible! | Ephesians 2:2-9 |

Forgiveness is a commandment from God to his children. "Forgive us our debts as we forgive our debtors". *Matthew 6:12*. Families have been shattered because of the lack of forgiveness. May you discover the power of forgiveness as demonstrated in the life of our Lord and Savior Jesus Christ.

## Praying for your family! Action Plan!

| Prayer Guide | Key scripture: Psalms 139 | Notes |
|---|---|---|
| Topic | You are fearfully and wonderfully made. | |
| Example: Family | Once you have chosen the topic, then determine the duration of the prayer. | God created family for His glory. Matthew 19:1-12 |
| How long will you pray? | The duration will depend on the need of your family. This is a continuous activity to pray for your family. | |
| Is there a need? | Assess the need-then make an action plan. | |
| What is the vision for your children -and Children's spouse? | The man determines the vision of his family. A family without a vision will not succeed. Pray for your husband, wife, children, and in-laws. | *Proverbs 29:18* |

Call unto me and I will answer you. *Jeremiah 33:3*. God will provide your daily bread.
Scriptures: *Matthew 6:11, Proverbs 22:6, Ephesians 6:4*. Choose one scripture above to pray for your children.
- Model: Our Lord's Prayer or sentence prayers. Luke 11. Also, you can use **ACTS** model: Experiencing a new beginning. (Bishop Calvin Bethea. Page 39)

**A**: Adore and worship

**C**: Confession of sin and disobedience

**T**: Thanksgiving for all He has done in your life

**S**: Supplication (praying for your needs and the needs of others)

**Duration of Prayer**: This will depend on the need of your family.

- **Action Plan**: Assess your family's need.
- Train your children with skills needed to be successful in life.
- Provide a safe and supportive environment for learning for your children.
- Develop daily communication with your family to assess any learning and social dysfunctionalities.
- Is there any generational sin? Identify it and set a time to pray to demolish any strongholds.
- Research institutions which are best for your children's education.
- Make a list of mentors to connect with. If this problem is emotional, meditate on how to control your anger, the problem and hand over the issue to God. Seek professional help.

Lord, I pray for _____. Name the child, problem and skills needed.

If the problem is emotional name the problem to God. Use warfare prayers. Ask Him for help and be specific.

Do you have anything to confess about your children or family? Tell God during your prayer time.

Evening: Meditate on these scriptures: *Number 14:18, Joshua chapter 1*.

What must you change? Do you need a day's retreat to discuss more with your child or a family member?

Did God speak to you? Did you obey him?

## Is there a problem in your life with money management ? Action Plan.

| Prayer Guide | Key scripture: *1 Timothy 6:10* | Notes |
|---|---|---|
| **Topic** | Deliverance from the love of money. | |
| Example: Finances/ Food | It is the root of all kinds of evil. God should provide for our daily needs. | *Matthew 6:13 Matthew 6:11* |
| How long will you pray? | The duration will depend on your need. | |
| Is there a need? Are you financially stable? | Assess the need - then make an action plan. | |
| What is the vision for your finances? What is your plan to be debt free? | The man determines the vison of his family. Where there is no vision the people perish. *Proverbs 29:18* | *Habakkuk 2:2, Proverbs 22:7* Write down each step to take. |

Call unto me and I will answer you. *Jeremiah 33:3*

Model: *Philippians 4:19. Scriptures: Proverbs 22:7, Ephesians 6:4*

Choose a quiet place to pray and use one of the scriptures above to pray about your finances.
 How did you get into debt?

Lord, I pray for _____ Name the problem, making the determination to be debt-free. You might want to use warfare prayers and try to change your career or pursue a path to financial freedom. Ask Him for help - and be specific.

Morning: Choose the right time to be alone and pray. Search for opportunities to be debt free. What is your vision for retirement?

Do you have any sin to confess? Cut all unwanted credit cards. Did you obey God?

Evening: Meditate on how to get out of debt. List the name of everyone you owe.

Duration: This might take a longer time to come up with a plan of action.

What do you have to change? Did God speak to you? Did you obey him?

# Is there a problem with your health? Action Plan!

| Prayer Guide | Key Scripture: *Psalms 91:10* No Harm shall overcome you. | Notes |
|---|---|---|
| Topic | *Exodus 15:26*. I am the Lord, your healer. *Psalms 121:7* | God is the only perfect healer. |
| Example: Children's health | God should protect your children from sexually transmitted diseases. Follow vaccination plans for your children. | Teach your children about sexually transmitted diseases and the impact it has on their lives and destiny. |
| Example: Your health | List all health problems If you have an infectious disease, follow all preventive measures. Make an appointment with your doctor. | Prevention is better than cure. List one preventive measure you will work on each week. |
| Action Plan and duration: | Follow proper preventive measures: hand-washing, Take your medication as prescribed until finished. Duration depends on your situation | Write a checklist to use as a guide on substances that are detrimental to your health. |

| What is the vision for your health? | How many times do you exercise per day? How is your heart health? What are your blood pressure goals? | Each week, write down your goals: e.g., BP, Cholesterol, A1c, blood sugar. |
|---|---|---|
| **Cicle One**: MD, Surgeon, Dentist, Pharmacy Doctor (Pharm.D) (DNP) Doctor of Nursing Practice (DPT) Doctor of Physical Therapy PA: Physician Assistant OT: Occupational Therapist RT: Respiratory Therapist SP: Speech Therapist Pathologist, Radialogist, Optometrist, Technologist, Spiritual Care Provider, | Chiropractor, Natural Medicine Practitioner, Herbalist, Nurses and Assitants, Pharm.Techs, Psychologists, etc. Topic: Pray for the health care professional for the following: 1.Wisdom 2.Compassion 3.Knowlegde 4.Safety issues 5.Prevention of error 6.Right procedure, right patient, right medication etc. 7.Pray for your pharmacist and nurse. | Make a check-list according to your need. Every appointment and procedure should be commited to the Lord before the day of the procedure. - Pray for the health care worker representing the company. - Let your prayer team take care of the request. - Pray for your doctor and his team. |

# Chapter Nine
# The Parable of the Ten Virgins

*"In the Lord's Prayer, the first petition is for daily bread. No one can worship God or love his neighbor on an empty stomach."* —**Woodrow Wilson**

*Bible Reading: Matthew 25:1-13 (ESV)*

> [1] *Then the kingdom of heaven will be like ten virgins who took their lamps and went to meet the bridegroom.* [2] *Five of them were foolish, and five were wise.* [3] *For when the foolish took their lamps, they took no oil with them,* [4] *but the wise took flasks of oil with their lamps.* [5] *As the bridegroom was delayed, they all became drowsy and slept.* [6] *But at midnight there was a cry, 'Here is the bridegroom! Come out to meet him.'* [7] *Then all those virgins rose and trimmed their lamps.* [8] *And the foolish said to the wise, 'Give us some of your oil, for our lamps are going out.'* [9] *But the wise answered, saying, 'Since there will not be enough for us and for you, go rather to the dealers and buy for yourselves.'* [10] *And while they were going to buy, the bridegroom came, and those who were ready went in with him to the marriage feast, and the door was shut.* [11] *Afterward the other virgins came also, saying, 'Lord, lord, open to us.'* [12] *But he answered,*

*'Truly, I say to you, I do not know you.'* [13] *Watch therefore, for you know neither the day nor the hour.*

## Signs of the End of the Age. *Matthew 24:3-14 (ESV)*

[3]" *As he sat on the Mount of Olives, the disciples came to him privately, saying, "Tell us, when will these things be, and what will be the sign of your coming and of the end of the age?"* [4] *And Jesus answered them, "See that no one leads you astray.* [5] *For many will come in my name, saying, 'I am the Christ,' and they will lead many astray.* [6] *And you will hear of wars and rumors of wars. See that you are not alarmed, for this must take place, but the end is not yet.* [7] *For nation will rise against nation, and kingdom against kingdom, and there will be famines and earthquakes in various places.* [8] *All these are but the beginning of the birth pains.*

[9] *"Then they will deliver you up to tribulation and put you to death, and you will be hated by all nations for my name's sake.* [10] *And then many will fall away and betray one another and hate one another.* [11] *And many false prophets will arise and lead many astray.* [12] *And because lawlessness will be increased, the love of many will grow cold.* [13] *But the one who endures to the end will be saved.* [14] *And this gospel of the kingdom will be proclaimed throughout the whole world as a testimony to all nations, and then the end will come.*

## Discussion:

Background: In my culture (Kom, Cameroon), the bride is escorted to meet the groom in his compound the night before the wedding. Before the ceremony takes place, there is an event called "Knock Door," when the groom visits with his family to ask for the bride's hand. Firewood, bags of salt, gallons of palm oil and all the necessary gifts are presented before the wedding can be performed. The bride is escorted to meet the groom at night with her face covered, adorned with precious jewels. In the story of the Ten Virgins, Jesus described how the Bridegroom came when everyone was sleeping.

## Questions for Group Study:

1. Reflect and state a tradition from your culture on how weddings are performed and how the bride prepares to meet the bridegroom.
2. Who is a virgin?
3. Why did Jesus use this scenario of virgins to address His disciples?
4. In *Matthew 24*, the disciples demanded a sign from Jesus, but how did He answer them in *Matthew 25:1-2*?
5. What word did Christ use to describe the Virgins?

6. What happened to the bridegroom on his way?

7. What happened to the Virgins while the bridegroom tarried?

   *Romans 12:1-2:* How do we wait or prepare for our Lord's coming today?

8. What is the significance of the lamb, the oil, and their virginity?

9. When did the bridegroom come, and what happened?

   *Bible Reading: Matthew 25:10-13*

   > [10]*And while they were going to buy, the bridegroom came, and those who were ready went in with him to the marriage feast, and the door was shut.* [11] *Afterward the other virgins came also, saying, 'Lord, lord, open to us.'* [12] *But he answered, 'Truly, I say to you, I do not know you.'* [13] *Watch therefore, for you know neither the day nor the hour.*

   ○ Why did the groom shut the door?
   ○ Who is the door? *John 10:9*

10. How did the Virgins call their master?
    ○ Read: *Matthew 7:21-23*
    ○ *Luke 6:46*
    ○ Why do we call him "Lord," but don't obey Him?
    ○ Is He truly LORD of our lives?
    ○ "I never knew you" meant **NO** intimacy with God – *only lip service.* *Matthew 7:21-23*

Jesus called those who performed great signs and miracles "workers of iniquity." In other words, to enter the kingdom of God, we must practice going to Christ daily and asking for forgiveness.

*1John 1:6-7,* daily self-denial and daily repentance. What sins easily beset us? The five foolish virgins procrastinated and were shut out from the heavenly banquet.

# Chapter Ten

# Jesus Prayed for His disciples and Future Disciples

*"Prayer is God's backstage pass into a personal audience with Him."* —**Tony Evans**

*Bible Reading: John 17: 6- 26 (ESV)*

[6] *"I have manifested your name to the people whom you gave me out of the world. Yours they were, and you gave them to me, and they have kept your word.* [7] *Now they know that everything that you have given me is from you.* [8] *For I have given them the words that you gave me, and they have received them and have come to know in truth that I came from you; and they have believed that you sent me.* [9] *I am praying for them. I am not praying for the world but for those whom you have given me, for they are yours.* [10] *All mine are yours, and yours are mine, and I am glorified in them.* [11] *And I am no longer in the world, but they are in the world, and I am coming to you. Holy Father, keep them in your name, which you have given me, that they may be one, even as we are one.* [12] *While I was with them, I kept them in your name, which you have given me. I have guarded them, and not one of them has been lost except the son of destruction, that the Scripture might be fulfilled.* [13] *But now I am coming to you, and these things I speak in the world, that they may have my*

*joy fulfilled in themselves.* [14] *I have given them your word, and the world has hated them because they are not of the world, just as I am not of the world.* [15] *I do not ask that you take them out of the world, but that you keep them from the evil one.* [16] *They are not of the world, just as I am not of the world.* [17] *Sanctify them in the truth; your word is truth.* [18] *As you sent me into the world, so I have sent them into the world.* [19] *And for their sake I consecrate myself, that they also may be sanctified in truth.*

[20] *"I do not ask for these only, but also for those who will believe in me through their word,* [21] *that they may all be one, just as you, Father, are in me, and I in you, that they also may be in us, so that the world may believe that you have sent me.* [22] *The glory that you have given me I have given to them, that they may be one even as we are one,* [23] *I in them and you in me, that they may become perfectly one, so that the world may know that you sent me and loved them even as you loved me.* [24] *Father, I desire that they also, whom you have given me, may be with me where I am, to see my glory that you have given me because you loved me before the foundation of the world.* [25] *O righteous Father, even though the world does not know you, I know you, and these know that you have sent me.* [26] *I made known to them your name, and I will continue to make it known, that the love with which you have loved me may be in them, and I in them."*

What can we learn from the above prayer on how Jesus prayed for his disciples?

# Chapter Eleven

# Paul's Prayer for the Ephesian Church

*"Prayer is our invitation to God to intervene in the affairs of earth. It is our request for Him to work His ways in this world."* —**Myles Munroe**

*Bible Reading: Ephesians 1:15-23 (ESV)*

[15] *For this reason, because I have heard of your faith in the Lord Jesus and your love toward all the saints,* [16] *I do not cease to give thanks for you, remembering you in my prayers,* [17] *that the God of our Lord Jesus Christ, the Father of glory, may give you the Spirit of wisdom and of revelation in the knowledge of him,* [18] *having the eyes of your hearts enlightened, that you may know what is the hope to which he has called you, what are the riches of his glorious inheritance in the saints,* [19] *and what is the immeasurable greatness of his power toward us who believe, according to the working of his great might* [20] *that he worked in Christ when he raised him from the dead and seated him at his right hand in the heavenly places,* [21] *far above all rule and authority and power and dominion, and above every name that is named, not only in this age but also in the one to come.* [22] *And he put all things under his feet and gave him as head over all things to the church,* [23] *which is his body, the fullness of him who fills all in all.*

Paul prayed for the church and other Christians. May the above prayer assist you with your prayer life.

# Chapter Twelve

# Daniel's Prayer During Spiritual Warfare

"Spiritual warfare is very real. There is a
furious, fierce, and ferocious battle raging in the
realm of the spirit between the forces of God
and the forces of evil. Warfare happens every
day, all the time. Whether you believe it or not,
you are in a battlefield. You are in warfare."
**—Pedro Okoro**

*Bible Reading: Daniel Chapter 9 (ESV)*

*¹ In the first year of Darius the son of Ahasuerus, by
descent a Mede, who was made king over the realm of
the Chaldeans— ² in the first year of his reign, I, Daniel,
perceived in the books the number of years that, according
to the word of the LORD to Jeremiah the prophet, must
pass before the end of the desolations of Jerusalem,
namely, seventy years.*

*³ Then I turned my face to the Lord God, seeking him
by prayer and pleas for mercy with fasting and sackcloth
and ashes. ⁴ I prayed to the LORD my God and made
confession, saying, "O Lord, the great and awesome God,
who keeps covenant and steadfast love with those who love
him and keep his commandments, ⁵ we have sinned and*

*done wrong and acted wickedly and rebelled, turning aside from your commandments and rules.* [6] *We have not listened to your servants the prophets, who spoke in your name to our kings, our princes, and our fathers, and to all the people of the land.* [7] *To you, O Lord, belongs righteousness, but to us open shame, as at this day, to the men of Judah, to the inhabitants of Jerusalem, and to all Israel, those who are near and those who are far away, in all the lands to which you have driven them, because of the treachery that they have committed against you.* [8] *To us, O* LORD, *belongs open shame, to our kings, to our princes, and to our fathers, because we have sinned against you.* [9] *To the Lord our God belong mercy and forgiveness, for we have rebelled against him* [10] *and have not obeyed the voice of the* LORD *our God by walking in his laws, which he set before us by his servants the prophets.* [11] *All Israel has transgressed your law and turned aside, refusing to obey your voice. And the curse and oath that are written in the Law of Moses the servant of God have been poured out upon us, because we have sinned against him.* [12] *He has confirmed his words, which he spoke against us and against our rulers who ruled us, by bringing upon us a great calamity. For under the whole heaven there has not been done anything like what has been done against Jerusalem.*

[13] *As it is written in the Law of Moses, all this calamity has come upon us; yet we have not entreated the favor of the* LORD *our God, turning from our iniquities and gaining insight by your truth.* [14] *Therefore the* LORD *has kept ready the calamity and has brought it upon us, for*

the LORD our God is righteous in all the works that he has done, and we have not obeyed his voice. [15] And now, O Lord our God, who brought your people out of the land of Egypt with a mighty hand, and have made a name for yourself, as at this day, we have sinned, we have done wickedly. [16] "O Lord, according to all your righteous acts, let your anger and your wrath turn away from your city Jerusalem, your holy hill, because for our sins, and for the iniquities of our fathers, Jerusalem and your people have become a byword among all who are around us. [17] Now therefore, O our God, listen to the prayer of your servant and to his pleas for mercy, and for your own sake, O Lord, make your face to shine upon your sanctuary, which is desolate. [18] O my God, incline your ear and hear. Open your eyes and see our desolations, and the city that is called by your name. For we do not present our pleas before you because of our righteousness, but because of your great mercy. [19] O Lord, hear; O Lord, forgive. O Lord, pay attention and act. Delay not, for your own sake, O my God, because your city and your people are called by your name."

## Gabriel Brings an Answer

[20] While I was speaking and praying, confessing my sin and the sin of my people Israel, and presenting my plea before the LORD my God for the holy hill of my God, [21] while I was speaking in prayer, the man Gabriel, whom I had seen in the vision at the first, came to me in swift flight at the time of the evening sacrifice. [22] He made me understand,

*speaking with me and saying, "O Daniel, I have now come out to give you insight and understanding.* [23] *At the beginning of your pleas for mercy a word went out, and I have come to tell it to you, for you are greatly loved. Therefore, consider the word and understand the vision.*

### The Seventy Weeks

[24] *"Seventy weeks are decreed about your people and your holy city, to finish the transgression, to put an end to sin, and to atone for iniquity, to bring in everlasting righteousness, to seal both vision and prophet, and to anoint a most holy place.* [25] *Know therefore and understand that from the going out of the word to restore and build Jerusalem to the coming of an anointed one, a prince, there shall be seven weeks. Then for sixty-two weeks it shall be built again with squares and moat, but in a troubled time.* [26] *And after the sixty-two weeks, an anointed one shall be cut off and shall have nothing. And the people of the prince who is to come shall destroy the city and the sanctuary. Its end shall come with a flood, and to the end there shall be war. Desolations are decreed.* [27] *And he shall make a strong covenant with many for one week, and for half of the week he shall put an end to sacrifice and offering. And on the wing of abominations shall come one who makes desolate, until the decreed end is poured out on the desolator."*

May the above prayer assist you with warfare prayers.

# Chapter Thirteen
# Hannah's Prayer for a Child

*"My mother was a Sunday school teacher. So I am a byproduct of prayer. My mom just kept on praying for her son."* —**Steve Harvey**

*Bible Reading: 1 Samuel 1: 1-28 (ESV)*

¹*There was a certain man of Ramathaim-zophim of the hill country of Ephraim whose name was Elkanah the son of Jeroham, son of Elihu, son of Tohu, son of Zuph, an Ephrathite.* ² *He had two wives. The name of the one was Hannah, and the name of the other, Peninnah. And Peninnah had children, but Hannah had no children.* ³ *Now this man used to go up year by year from his city to worship and to sacrifice to the* LORD *of hosts at Shiloh, where the two sons of Eli, Hophni and Phinehas, were priests of the* LORD. ⁴ *On the day when Elkanah sacrificed, he would give portions to Peninnah his wife and to all her sons and daughters.* ⁵ *But to Hannah he gave a double portion, because he loved her, though the* LORD *had closed her womb.* ⁶ *And her rival used to provoke her grievously to irritate her, because the* LORD *had closed her womb.* ⁷ *So it went on year by year. As often as she went up to the house of the* LORD, *she used to provoke her. Therefore, Hannah wept and would not eat.* ⁸ *And Elkanah, her husband, said to her, "Hannah, why do you weep? And why do you*

not eat? And why is your heart sad? Am I not more to you than ten sons?'"

⁹ After they had eaten and drunk in Shiloh, Hannah rose. Now Eli the priest was sitting on the seat beside the doorpost of the temple of the LORD. ¹⁰ She was deeply distressed and prayed to the LORD and wept bitterly. ¹¹ And she vowed a vow and said, "O LORD of hosts, if you will indeed look on the affliction of your servant and remember me and not forget your servant, but will give to your servant a son, then I will give him to the LORD all the days of his life, and no razor shall touch his head."

¹² As she continued praying before the LORD, Eli observed her mouth. ¹³ Hannah was speaking in her heart; only her lips moved, and her voice was not heard. Therefore, Eli took her to be a drunken woman. ¹⁴ And Eli said to her, "How long will you go on being drunk? Put your wine away from you." ¹⁵ But Hannah answered, "No, my lord, I am a woman troubled in spirit. I have drunk neither wine nor strong drink, but I have been pouring out my soul before the LORD. ¹⁶ Do not regard your servant as a worthless woman, for all along I have been speaking out of my great anxiety and vexation." ¹⁷ Then Eli answered, "Go in peace, and the God of Israel grant your petition that you have made to him." ¹⁸ And she said, "Let your servant find favor in your eyes." Then the woman went her way and ate, and her face was no longer sad.

[19] *They rose early in the morning and worshiped before the* LORD; *then they went back to their house at Ramah. And Elkanah knew Hannah his wife, and the* LORD *remembered her.* [20] *And in due time Hannah conceived and bore a son, and she called his name Samuel, for she said, "I have asked for him from the* LORD." *Samuel Given to the* LORD.[21] *The man Elkanah and all his house went up to offer to the* LORD *the yearly sacrifice and to pay his vow.* [22] *But Hannah did not go up, for she said to her husband, "As soon as the child is weaned, I will bring him, so that he may appear in the presence of the* LORD *and dwell there forever."* [23] *Elkanah her husband said to her, "Do what seems best to you; wait until you have weaned him; only, may the* LORD *establish his word." So the woman remained and nursed her son until she weaned him.* [24] *And when she had weaned him, she took him up with her, along with a three-year-old bull, an ephah of flour, and a skin of wine, and she brought him to the house of the* LORD *at Shiloh. And the child was young.* [25] *Then they slaughtered the bull, and they brought the child to Eli.* [26] *And she said, "Oh, my lord! As you live, my lord, I am the woman who was standing here in your presence, praying to the* LORD. [27] *For this child I prayed, and the* LORD *has granted me my petition that I made to him.* [28] *Therefore I have lent him to the* LORD. *As long as he lives, he is lent to the* LORD." *And he worshiped the* LORD *there.*

- **Who were the distractors in Hannah's life?**
- **How did Hannah overcome her storm?**

May the above scriptures and prayers assist you to be persistent in prayer.

# Chapter Fourteen

# A Prayer of Repentance by King David

*"A man walks on through life - with the external call ringing in his ears but with no response stirring in his heart, and then suddenly, without any warning, the Spirit taps him on the shoulder. What happens? He turns 'round. The word 'repentance' means 'turning 'round.' He repents and believes and is saved."*
**—Peter Marshall**

This prayer should be part of every Christian's prayer life. King David had sinned against God by committing adultery and murder. He hid his sin and intentionally placed Uriah - husband of the woman David had committed adultery with - on the front-line battle to be killed. David's sin was a secret, but the Lord God revealed this action to his prophet, Nathan, who confronted David. (*2 Sam. 12*). When the prophet delivered the message to David, that the child born in this adulterous relationship would die, David's convictions prompted him to pray for repentance. *Psalms 51*. King David poured his heart before God and asked for forgiveness, which involved confession and repentance. David did exactly what God requires of us. Do you have sin in your life? Have you made Christ Lord of your life? If not, here is the opportunity to stop now, confess your sins, and believe that Jesus is the son of God, crucified on the cross for you and me. *1 John 1:9* states, "If we confess our sins, He is faithful and just to forgive all our sins and cleanse us from all unrighteousness." Jesus can do the same for you.

*Bible Reading: Psalms 51 (ESV)*

*Have mercy on me, O God,*
*    according to your steadfast love;*
*according to your abundant mercy*
*    blot out my transgressions.*
*2 Wash me thoroughly from my iniquity,*
*    and cleanse me from my sin!*

*3 For I know my transgressions,*
*    and my sin is ever before me.*
*4 Against you, you only, have I sinned*
*    and done what is evil in your sight,*
*so that you may be justified in your words*
*    and blameless in your judgment.*
*5 Behold, I was brought forth in iniquity,*
*    and in sin did my mother conceive me.*
*6 Behold, you delight in truth in the inward being,*
*    and you teach me wisdom in the secret heart.*

[7] *Purge me with hyssop, and I shall be clean;*
  *wash me, and I shall be whiter than snow.*
[8] *Let me hear joy and gladness;*
  *let the bones that you have broken rejoice.*
[9] *Hide your face from my sins,*
  *and blot out all my iniquities.*
[10] *Create in me a clean heart, O God,*
  *and renew a right spirit within me.*
[11] *Cast me not away from your presence,*
  *and take not your Holy Spirit from me.*
[12] *Restore to me the joy of your salvation,*
  *and uphold me with a willing spirit.*

[13] *Then I will teach transgressors your ways,*
  *and sinners will return to you.*
[14] *Deliver me from blood guiltiness, O God,*
  *O God of my salvation,*
  *and my tongue will sing aloud of your righteousness.*
[15] *O Lord, open my lips,*
  *and my mouth will declare your praise.*
[16] *For you will not delight in sacrifice, or I would give it;*
  *you will not be pleased with a burnt offering.*
[17] *The sacrifices of God are a broken spirit;*
  *a broken and contrite heart, O God, you will not despise.*

[18] *Do good to Zion in your good pleasure;*
  *build up the walls of Jerusalem;*

$^{19}$ *then will you delight in right sacrifices,*
  *in burnt offerings and whole burnt offerings;*
  *then bulls will be offered on your altar.*

**Have you ever prayed with all emotions like King David?**

**What can we learn about God's character from this prayer?**

# Chapter Fifteen
# Nehemiah's Prayer

*"If any of you should ask me for an epitome of the Christian religion, I should say that it is in one word - prayer. Live and die without prayer, and you will pray long enough when you get to hell."*
**—Charles Spurgeon**

*Bible Reading: Nehemiah Chapter 1:1-11 (ESV)*

[1] *Now it happened in the month of Chislev, in the twentieth year, as I was in Susa the citadel,* [2] *that Hanani, one of my brothers, came with certain men from Judah. And I asked them concerning the Jews who escaped, who had survived the exile, and concerning Jerusalem.* [3] *And they said to me, "The remnant there in the province who had survived the exile is in great trouble and shame. The wall of Jerusalem is broken down, and its gates are destroyed by fire."*

*Nehemiah's Prayer* [4] *As soon as I heard these words I sat down and wept and mourned for days, and I continued fasting and praying before the God of heaven.* [5] *And I said, "O LORD God of heaven, the great and awesome God who keeps covenant and steadfast love with those who love him and keep his commandments,* [6] *let your ear be attentive and your eyes open, to hear the prayer of your servant that I now pray before you day and night for the people of Israel your servants, confessing the sins of the people of Israel, which we have sinned against you. Even I and my father's house have sinned.* [7] *We have acted very corruptly against you and have not kept the command-ments, the statutes, and the rules that you commanded your servant Moses.* [8] *Remember the word that you commanded your servant Moses, saying, 'If you are unfaithful, I will scatter you among the peoples,* [9] *but if you return to me and keep my commandments and do them, though your outcasts are in the uttermost parts of heaven, from there I will gather them and bring them to the place that I have chosen, to make my name dwell there.'* [10] *They are your servants and your people, whom you have redeemed by your great power and by your strong hand.* [11] *O Lord, let your ear be attentive to the prayer of your servant, and to the prayer of your servants who delight to fear your name, and give success to your servant today, and grant him mercy in the sight of this man." Now I was cupbearer to the king.*

## How can this prayer help us to pray for our nation?

## Who was Nehemiah?

## How has God placed you strategically for His purpose?

## How did Nehemiah react to the news about his nation?

# Chapter Sixteen
# Prayer Guide for Your Health

*"All the money in the world can't buy you back good health."* —**Reba McEntire**

The Merriam Webster dictionary defines health as " the condition of being sound in body, mind or spirit, especially or freedom from physical disease or pain." Our health is one of the most important gifts we have on earth. As Christians, we need to pray for good health. This concept is indirectly included in the Lord's Prayer. When we pray for our daily bread, we also need to pray for foods that are healthy for our bodies. If we eat unhealthy food, we will suffer the consequences of that choice. Throughout scripture, God has instructed his children on what and how to eat and drink. If we consume substances full of saturated fat and foods that are toxic to our bodies, we will eventually develop diseases that might be debilitating to us and to our families.

- "Whether therefore ye eat or drink, or whatsoever ye do, do all to the glory of God." KJV. *1 Corinthians 10:31*. We have to be healthy in order to carry out our daily activites on earth. Jesus spent most of his life on earth performing miracles and curing diseases. *John 9:5-7*. His desire for you is to discover His healing power in your life.

- "He who lacks wisdom should ask God who gives generously without finding fault, and it will be given to you." KJV. *James 1:5*
- God was the first surgeon on earth, performing the first surgery when he put Adam into sleep to fashion his wife. *Genesis 2:22*.
- God created medicinal plants for our benefits and to heal our diseases.
- We must discover Him to learn instructions on how to live a healthy life like the woman with the issue of blood. *Luke 8:43-48*

### Prayers for our Health should be Categorized into Non-infectious Diseases and Infectious Diseases

Non-infectious diseases are not contagious or inherited, but are often encountered due to socio-economic status, lifestyle, stress, trauma, and environmental factors. Sometimes, cultural background can precipitate an unheathy lifestyle, resulting in the development of all kinds of medical problems. Minimal knowledge of basic diseases is vital as we pray for our health and the health of others. During Biblical times, Hezekiah prayed to God, asking for long life. *2 Kings 20:1-11*. King Hezekiah was sick and God healed him - adding 15 years to his life. Below are some points to consider when praying:

- Pray for wisdom to consume and maintain proper nutrition.
- Wisdom to drink healthy drinks.
- Ability to exercise at least 30 minutes per day.
- Deliverance from the evil of toxic substances such as cigarettes and illegal drugs.
- Smoking cessation will decrease your blood pressure, prevent heart disease, and cancer.

    One person dies every 37[1] seconds in the United States from heart disease so, pray that you will have the knowledge to prevent heart diseases by decreasing the consumption of salty diets and foods high in cholesterol content.
- Learn to decrease the consumption of foods with a high sugar content.
- Follow up with your yearly appointments with your healthcare providers.
- Consult your pharmacist before taking any over-the-counter medication together

with a prescription drug to prevent drug-drug interactions, which might be fatal to your health.

- Pursue ways to prevent obesity.
- He who walks with the wise will be wise but the companion of fools will suffer harm. *Proverbs 13:20 (NKJV)*

# Infectious Diseases

*"By recognizing that infectious disease is not some faraway exotic issue but a global problem, and by sharing the responsibility for its prevention, diagnosis, and control, the whole world will be a lot safer."*
**—Seth Berkley**

Bacteria, virus, or fungus cause an infectious disease. These organisms can transmit infections through human blood, air, or direct contact with individuals who have the disease. We are living in perilous times with a pandemic called COVID-19, caused by the coronavirus. To pray effectively for individuals to combat this disease, we must follow instructions on how to prevent the spread of coronavirus.

Since the Influenza pandemic in 1918, the world had never seen a pandemic such as COVID-19. Fifty million individuals died worldwide during the flu pandemic[2]. While scientists are searching for a cure for the Coronavirus, preventing the spread of the disease is the best medicine.

Below is a link to guidelines from the Center for Disease Control (CDC) to assist you and your community.

https://www.cdc.gov/coronavirus/2019-ncov/
hcp/guidance-prevent-spread.html

## Steps to Protect Yourself from Coronavirus[3]

- Hand-washing with soap and water for at
  least 20 seconds
- Rub hands completely with hand sanitizer
  if there is no soap and water
- Do not cough with your mouth open,
  cough toward your elbow
- After touching any surface, make sure you
  wash your hands
- Do not touch your eyes, nose, or mouth
  with unclean hands
- Practice social distancing with others - do
  not shake hands
- Wear a mask if you are sick and are
  around other people
- Clean and disinfect areas that are
  frequently used in your house and place
  of work
- Hand-washing is one of the best steps in
  preventing this disease

***When to seek medical help*** - Seek help when
you are experiencing the following:

- Chest pain or pressure in the chest
- Bluish lips or face

- Difficulty breathing

In *Leviticus chapter 26*, the Lord threatens his people with a plague, including symptoms of fever and wasting of the body. He instituted an action plan for His people to implement to be delivered from this plague; God wanted his children to obey His commands so that they would no longer be slaves. When we refuse to obey God's commands, our land and cities will lie in ruins. *Leviticus 26:33*. God allows plagues to enable his people to call unto Him. While God could decide to heal everyone at His will, He has given us a standard by which we must live to stay healthy. His Word has all the instructions we need regarding safety and deliverance from plagues and illness.

# God Initiated Quarantine

Quarantine is an effective way of inhibiting an infectious disease in any community or nation.

*Leviticus 13:46.* "He shall remain unclean all the days during which has the infection; he is unclean. He shall live alone; his dwelling shall be outside the camp." In Biblical times, individuals were quarantined for seven days to eliminate the disease. *Leviticus 13:2-5, Luke 17:12, Numbers 5:2.* Quarantine enables the community and society to prevent the spread of some infectious diseases from person to person. Other infections diseases, such as sexually transmitted diseases, can be overcome by abstinence or using protective measures to prevent them. Sexually transmitted disease (STD) could affect your marriage, your family, and destroy your legacy.

There are numerous types of STD, but I have listed the most common types:

- Human Immunodeficiency Virus (HIV-AIDS) has devastated the world's population.
- Gonorrhea and syphilis have adversely affected individuals who plan to start a family.

- Genital herpes and trichomoniasis can cause birth defects in newborns.
- Hepatitis C Virus (HCV) can destroy the liver.

These are serious diseases that warrant serious preventive measures. If individuals initiate such measures, our communities will enjoy peace and joy – the benefits of living a healthy lifestyle.

While antibiotics can be used to treat STDs caused by bacteria, they are not effective on those caused by a virus. Malaria and Tuberculosis (TB)[4,5] can be prevented by avoiding environments with the parasite. Malaria is caused by infection from mosquitoes, while TB is caused by an infection from bacteria or a virus. Contact with individuals who have this disease is devastating to families and communities, but there are medications and vaccines available to stop the spread of malaria and TB. Human papillomavirus (HPV) can cause cancer of genital organs. More information can be found within the CDC guidelines below.[6]

As we pray for our health, we need to be wise to follow all preventive measures and instructions regarding the right vaccines, medications and medicinal plants to treat and cure diseases.

My people are destroyed because of a lack of knowledge. *Hosea 4:6*. This verse will transform the lives of all who are willing to humble themselves and learn about their health.

Many people from underdeveloped nations suffer from malaria and other infectious diseases, but basic knowledge of any disease (and medications used to treat it) can save thousands of lives. Doxycycline is a medication that is used for the prevention of malaria and the treatment of other infections; however, taking it with dairy products can affect it's eficacy. The body's infection will continue to increase and the effectiveness of the drug will decrease. When doxycycline is taken with antacids such as bismuth subsalicylate (Pepto-Bismol), it can decrease the bio- availability of Doxycycline by 37%- 51% percent. Take doxycycline 2 hours before any antacids.[7] Medications such as doxycycline, tetracycline, and ciprofloxacin should be taken 2 hours before or 4 hours after the consumption of any products containing calcium, magnesium, or aluminum.[8,9]

*A patient's lack of knowledge of drug-drug and drug-food interactions can be fatal.*

Therefore, never underestimate the power of proper hygiene and effective hand-washing in disease prevention. When we pray, we need an action plan that includes learning basic knowledge about illness, medications (and how to take them), as well as *when to get vaccinated* to prevent our bodies from developing diseases. Following proper measures will help us become victorious over physical, spiritual, or social problems in our families and communities.

Remember: Prayer is communication with God. *Jeremiah 30:17.* " I will give you back health and heal your wounds." Ask God for help - and be specific. LORD _____ [name of the person and the problem.] Ask God to deliver you or your child from _____ [state the disease.] For example, state the issue (STDs, heart disease, COVID-19, HIV-AIDS, substance disorders, diabetes, etc.), and let Him instill in the heart of the individual a desire to abstain from unhealthy behaviors. Choose a quiet place to pray, and if you are harboring any sins or unhealthy lifestyle, confess those to God, making sure to hear His voice, and obey His will.

Use the health prayer chart in chapter eight to assist you to pray for your health. Use one of the prayer samples and implement an action plan for your family, church, community, and nation. When we pray, we discover His attributes, His loving kindness, His Mercy and His power. God is perfect in all His ways. This should lead us to prostrate before him each time we experience Him in prayer.

We pray because the only way to be right with God is through communion with his Son. We come to Him with our needs - as demonstrated by our Lord Jesus. We pray for our daily bread, protection, and deliverance from evil - including deliverance from hell. Spiritual warfare is real, so we need to use prayer, which is the only offensive weapon we have to combat the wiles of the enemy. You can pray in a quiet place, or anywhere you find comfortable to fellowship with your Heavenly Father.

# Summary

Prayer is communication with God. God is a relational Being who created man in His own image to have fellowship with Him. He initiated communication when He created man in the Garden of Eden. During creation, He communicated by speaking the world into existence. For example, in *Genesis 1:3*, God said "Let there be light," and there was light. After God created man and woman, He communicated with them by giving specific instructions. *Genesis 2:16*. "You may eat of every tree in the Garden but the tree of knowledge of good and evil you may not eat of if, for the day you eat of it you may surely die." God taught man how to communicate because He brought the animals to Adam to name. God called Adam by name when he sinned.

Communication with God will reveal our identity, God's vision for us, and our destiny in life.

When we pray, we communicate with God who is our Heavenly Father and our Creator. We express our thoughts, gratitude, and our heart's desires to Him. We pray when there is a need, as the Spirit leads. God has invited us into a relationship with Him through His son, Christ Jesus. He is waiting for us to *come as we are*. He desires our praise, our worship, and honor - for He is a Holy God and all who come to Him must acknowledged His Holiness, glory, and majesty.

During prayer, we discover His will for our lives, His mercy, His love, forgiveness, and His compassion.

We approach God in humility, recognizing our sinfulness and accepting His forgiveness. Any posture is acceptable before God, whether it be kneeling, standing, or walking. God reveals His character to us, directing us in what we need to pray for, and how to pray. During prayer, we can call on the names of God as we honor and worship Him in prayer.

I pray this Prayer Guide will be a blessing to you and the body of Christ!

## References and Resources: Websites for more information:

1. Heart Disease Facts. (2019, December 2). Retrieved from https://www.cdc.gov/ heart-disease/facts.htm

2. https://www.cdc.gov/flu/pandemic-resources/ 1918-pandemic-h1n1.html

3. Coronavirus Disease 2019 (COVID-19). (n.d.). Retrieved from https://www.cdc. gov/corona-virus/2019-ncov/index.html

4. CDC - Parasites - Malaria. (2020, April 1). Retrieved from https://www.cdc.gov/ parasites/malaria/index.html

5. Basic TB facts. (2020, March 27). Centers for Disease Control and Prevention. Retrieved from https://www.cdc.gov/tb/topic/basics/ default.htm

6. HPV. (2019, August 15). Retrieved from https://www.cdc.gov/hpv/hcp/sched-ules-recommendations.html

7. Ericsson, C. D. "Influence of Subsalicylate Bismuth on Absorption of Doxycycline." *JAMA: The Journal of the American Medical Association*,

vol. 247, no. 16, 1982, pp. 2266–2267., doi: 10.1001/ jama.247.16.2266.

8. Barr, W. H., Adir, J., & Garrettson, L. (1971). Decrease of tetracycline absorption in man by sodium bicarbonate. *Clinical Pharmacology & Therapeutics*, 12 (5), 779–784. doi: 10.1002/ cpt1971125779

9. Arayne, M., Sultana, N., & Hussain, F. (2005). Interactions Between Ciprofloxacin and Antacids – *Dissolution and Adsorption Studies. Drug Metabolism and Drug Interactions*, 21(2). doi: 10.1515/dmdi. 2005.21.2.117

## Note about the Author:

Dr. Genet Azang-Njaah and her husband, Lucas Azang-Njaah, have been married for over 36 years. They have three children and two grandchildren. Genet has served as a short-term medical missionary, along with her husband, in the United States, South Africa, and Cameroon. She developed a passion for medical missions and women's work after graduating from the College of Pharmacy in 1991. Since then, she and her husband have served together in Missions and have organized leadership conferences, marriage workshops, retreats, and mentoring programs to encourage the Body of Christ. She and her husband are members of the Associate Reformed Presbyterian Church in America.

May this book help
you as you pray!

By Genet Azang-Njaah

# Notes

# Notes

# Notes

# Notes

# Commitment

Made in the USA
Columbia, SC
14 September 2022

67083018R00065